MW01479421

A Day in the Sun

José Argüelles Jan 24 1939-Mar 23 2011
Ivan Argüelles Jan 24 1939-

Poems

Ivan Argüelles

LUNA BISONTE PRODS

2012

A DAY IN THE SUN

© Ivan Argüelles 2012

Para mi hermana Laurita que nos cuidó a nosotros, los cuates, en las horas oscuras.

Front cover photo shows Ivan and José Argüelles
enjoying a day in the sun.
Back cover art and book design
by C. Mehrl Bennett.

10 digit ISBN: 1-892280-93-0

13 digit ISBN: 978-1-892280-93-0

LUNA BISONTE PRODS

137 Leland Ave.

Columbus, OH 43214 USA

http://www.lulu.com/spotlight/lunabisonteprods

www.johnmbennett.net

[Achilles in Hades]

red style archaic vase painting
now a lost postcard from the Metro-
politan who interrogates him if not
himself Agamemnon who got it unawares
in the bath tub a miasma indecorous
coming forth to address the Turks
on their recent victory in Anatolia
Thetis weeping long and mourning
on the sandy mount east of nowhere
what the oracular voice darkening
is her fair-haired still blood
dried over the mask of his fate
sobbing into her knees gasoline
drenched cloth where the diesel
broke down on the march up-country
as bats flitting blind the souls
of men released by the Fist invisible
chaos theory at best looking for

skin the song that best fits each
mine! shouts hoarsely into a phone
a brother lost in the hospital
of no return then denied light ex-
pires on a Tuesday before dawn
a tale as exiguous as it is blank
a winding down of smoke going up
in 19th century ether Theory a void
extended in their nets by Naiads
immortal for their watery beauty
a cast off beyond thundering shoals
the remains of the Hesperian lake
which nothing reflects back to the
++++++++++++++++++++++++++++++++++
archaic rudiments of speech alpha
bits a type of rumination animus
tenderloin his barking against Hector
who his love dragged in dusty gyres
round Ilium's cyclopean walls AOI
ponder nothing in the Library whole

2

afternoons in taffeta and silk dusk
passing notes in cuneiform back and
forth to the sphinx her mutilated
snout in the ancient sun basking
dumb and blind to the adverse heat
a laminated sheet erected against
the clinic's brassy carillon ringing
the Hours which none hear fighting
body to body in the violent welter
to conjugate the verbs rightly in-
spired to touch by art the firmament
accept this that it is dying every time
and not reversible though Memory's
tainted leaf tipped against the pane
freezes some dried evidence of green
in the resumption of blackness total
falls back then Thetis' son wounded
fatally by some cruel powdery dream
his not a circular verbatim but fierce
the injection of mind into matter

seeing in a rush all the stars that
have ever been such Bright between
the ears then soaked in Lethe's charm
oblivion resumes its twilight sheets
around the ruins of his shadowy form
a name at least to be recalled again
in a perhaps of cloudy paintings

05-22-11

siamo nati nel fango
e appena riusciamo a vedere
la luce che piove dal cielo

futility of existence
the last named street
of the roman empire
which requires tragedy
the lasting nothingness
of a stone falling nowhere
when suddenly a light
then a void an absence
where presumption flared
mud aches even as water
touched by night undergoes
a last transformation
the next time a poem
occurs or a window shakes
ever so slightly

darkness at the lip
of things fading forever
is it that memory is rain
nothing lasts as evidence
smoking to stay awake
held in the grip of a
vision brightly ephemeral
hold to no one thing
although voices are heard
their organization is infirm
like walls of sponge
one cannot sustain this
a labyrinth of cigarettes
named after certain women
who burned to know
who are in no one place now
who may never have been
at all
like a siege of space
the inchoate trembles

archaic matter descends
with the one desire to flame
the mind's plume goes up
witnessed by no one
sleep, then, sleep
(I am heavy, mother,
and have no place to go)

05-17-11

(for José)

where they draw evening out

a transparent god

   hewn from quartz

presides

         something

in the air

        a burnished frame

out of which issues

     Night with its

bright calligraphy of stars

   where the evening Hour spends

its must in pale

   in the air a

           Sound

whitens as if flesh

     falling from one

dream into the other

    to gather the grass

into a single heap
           a shadow
       what intensity!
at the core heat which
is the red of metamorphosis
       palpable as
who is it?
           flame that nurtures
           flame
if the half is dead
               then what?
to linger in thought
           tolling bells
where once was clear
           the song
   a world away
ashes nothing but
       strewn into
an empyrean august
       to what avail

numbers cardinal
    ordinal sign
a symbol in the Eye
  by the sea a
roaring shaft water
    of the depths
like the stygian promise
      who abides
  like a phantom vanishing
a brother an echo

07-08-11

[poem metaphysical]

how much doth Love its shadow
to sustain doth try
but mindful yet of Light
the darkness doth apply

so songs around the tomb do go
a chant of ancient solemnity
when shall we meet again
Thou and I shadows of perplexity?

foregone the other day a summer
long since revolved to dust
but still the sweetest chords
the voices' echoes waver must

hath the sun's once bright Eye
gone blind in sandstorms of the tomb
hath even moonlight surrendered
its sheen and glow in the blackest room?

alas my Soul your half doth wander
midst waters of pure oblivion
and I here on the world's bleak shore
a second half do mourn the fields Elysian

shepherd on the rock delightest once
thy pipe in crystal airs to sound
now mute in caverns labyrinthine deep
the silver rills fall sleeping underground

what heights once climbed the fleet of foot
and kenned Mind's hungry intellect
what vast then starry endlessness unfold
in remembrance of that sweet prospect

now the Hour hath nor sign nor wound
and the minutes turn to flight and sand
what hovers in the mirror's broken pane
if not the Shadow's long and empty hand

I long to go as well today into the Void
I here no more do pine to stay
nor for delights of worldly matter care
but to end this Note at once I say

and nevermore the Book consult
for distances of time and life
belief is a grimoire deaf and stoned
the Heart's a loss with sorrow rife

07-13-11

[sing O muse]

earth does not give us back
though effortless in the light
anemone hyacinth narcissus dog-wood
shower their fragrance of color
nothing of us returns from the fundament
nor flitting like bats do the shades
knocking against old furniture
in the dark take hold
nothing of substance remains
though the poet in his archaic voice
how longing becomes the day's
unique Hour sings that passage
melancholy and
how many times do You ask?
earth does not give us back
but out of each verse from us
removes a sense and rhyme
to make again a different world

not for us to behold
a dark rampart that separates
dream from dream
even as falling angels nightly
careen downwards against metal
thinking to have been that dream
osprey and gull take flight
no sooner does dawn mark
the invisible horizon with its dust
of spent stars and galaxies
earth does not give us back
nor does that love we held supreme
nor does any remnant of memory
green as the eternal grass
give us back to one another--
the chthonic deities
their small red eyes glowing
with malice scamper to their
etruscan mansions in a beyond
of sulphur and hematite

can they give us back?
[remember the boy next door
so shy and kind always obeyed
his mother now has blood on his hands
has history been to him any kinder?]
other lesser deities such as
minerva and mercury gloat
behind sand and brick that
nothing has come back
not the agony not the velvet
secret of love in disguise
not anything like grass or water
overlaying ancient cities
monotony of days without rhythm
sleeping by chance in ditches
or suddenly stepping up to
a microphone to recite hexameter
the vergilian heroine burnt to the core
apex of drumroll and quicksilver
earth does not give us back

+++++++++++++++++++++

by an archaic chinese canal
geese mysteriously arrayed
plum blossom scent to read
in the sky an omen
to surrender to a curtain
of incense and
situationism   business
of looping the ends to meet
a random bunch of flowers
from behind the willows a flute
yellow melody going lost
in mists

            identity

saturdays in the library head
heavy with the rhombus of echo
spelling defiance in a submerged
script to rephrase the enigma
pronouncing as brahmins the vedic
text until numb

            loss of value

circulating like a star out of its
ellipse dreaming yes the whiteness
of thighs breasts shoulders
pillowed against a massive cloud
being shaped for a storm
whipping sea into a
  albescent foam
      loss
small tributaries out to
where caulked the ships freshly
  wait for me
bronze ringing bronze
heralds black as pitch swinging
crosiers of daylight
in their eyes a similar landscape
fragmented breaks off
ruddy deities emergent
      mind
itself the illusory clay
to mould into supple peregrine

figures crossing like lightning
in the magnificent heaven of
childhood
earth does not give us back
nor the sonant glyphs
nor at breakneck speed Thought
+++++++++++++++++++++++++++
not give us back earth
the snot nosed kid named achilles
hell-bent an ochre dust haloes him
whom in delight the gods slay
give earth not back us
propelled like a blind aviator
into the enormous crepuscular flare
never tomorrow back
nor the flaked shells of memory
dizzy specters in the mausoleum
which houses the soul of the Sphinx
us never back earth give
not a nullity every friday

celebrated over the corpse of Osiris

odd shifts of time

can you see through That?

earth shifts time

until

07-16-11

(the poet)

how the poet organizes for his
own garden for his own feckless
dive below the soil for his for-
saken by god illumination by
the root of his hair pulled by
the Muse through the glass
into the distinctions of light
and the periphery limitless
night swans ululating a mass
eleison! each is one of us a
"the" without syntax re-
plete with the color Red a
sounding the water of thought
loud amaze of firth and reef
cut to the quick by suddenness
a life come full circle before
hotels where we met You and

your other me was a swoon
a dead ended adolescent privy
to scorn and elation by textual
adaptation the homeric blind
succumbed to the dust storms
which are the refugee's prayer
small deities of dark intuition
gone at once stoned in corridors
of illusion and something else
comes out of the grasses humming
the Soul that wayward thing
clinging to nothing a register
of notes the melody of Heaven
shadow play of flute and tin
whose head this is so heavy
a dreaming lark in Provence
to take flight a surge of words
to understand them! pity us
(eleison!) stark under rock
groping for the lintel the green

of living rapidly the tumescent
a verger dense with Mind
labyrinth of root and tragedy
iphigenia surrendered to the
Wave how harsh clouds intense
with purple the grafted Ire
surround all bedded innocence
to not wake the better to hold
the gate has fallen the Beyond
unpredicted by the gardener
his small buddha wish white
as the pebble of memory
remaining or not remaining
abysmal second thoughts about
in each row a certain tree
like letters of an alphabet
only the Poet kens relentless
against the wind leaning
a house is missing a pilgrim
a thin liquid spells Desire
in the rampant sky of organdy

everywhere it is futile
everywhere it is
hills just west of the way
cannot see more than that
a lesson in organizing
exactly what it is to die

07-18-11

(anatolia)

where poppies grow bright red
that men put to sleep
what is the form of separation?
what are the terms
coming to light going upcountry?
the baggage of memory listing
pack animals of dream like
immense shapes of dust burden
the Soul weaving pathless
haze and labyrinth the body
itself the Unknown
if rock crystal hewn from air
as it were and dim reminiscence
of the Isle a distance cool
and blank as opium
to render us null and void
the hand's numb chisel
working against some furious
entity who wraps around Being

cessation of identity
regard me as Orestes
swarming in some dark corridor
with bad conscience
for life was ever a regret
a symptom that rests in dying
this tuesday as on all such days
celebrate the trionfo della morte
as envisioned by the ten thousand
who will remember their names?
+++++++++++++++++++++++++++
the text compounded with error
whistles through the eaves
spelling disaster for the philosopher
from Miletus who first scanned
the empyrean with Number
the archaic voice hoarse
after millennia of calling out
or like the corpse dragged
countless times around the walls

of windy Ilium   amaze!
a decent pornography tracing
with a wet finger the terse
white thighs of the goddess
who in nonchalance smokes
half naked the Cigarette of chance
though her temple be a Ruin
the stones worn by circular fate
to a nothingness still her perfume
radiates in the scrub brush
intoxicating the god-weary Ionians
it is the search for the "what"?
the empire of language
has been deconstructed syllable
by pointless syllable
until exhausted in the loggia
we pass glances through a smoked lens
at the towering figure of Smoke
it is his destiny to defy!
even as the planet plunges
to its nadir

+++++++++++++++++++++++++

burning water
burning burning through the transom
no edge resists the flame
moon deposits her fade aspirin
it is the mountain where
like maggots we are buried
chattering ceaselessly about Parmenides
about the day of the Coup
when everything was a wall
when we could not come
to our senses   amaze!
the soles of the feet burning
the shadows of men
in their congress of syntax
gnats and horse-flies!
how is it the One
passes from this life to the next
without surrendering its unity?

7-19-11

28

(archaic)

silence that begets silence
                        in-
separable in heat
                climbing hill
vergers   lush green re-
    clining
                    on either
side   other
stone lain
                carefully upon
                stone a
hawk   distance
            cries   shrill
to make a temple
            where
                cool between
            her thighs
goddess   queen
            a hush

wave

      salt   foam

stepping out of which

      glistening

  skin   song

whitening hori-

       zon a-

zure   th'anomalous

    peering

       fuck

too hard

    each letter

  a design   heart

felt spun

    loom dark

  her Hair

      chestnut deep

lost in

    the Eye

  circling   circling

sand   a-

     maze   why

to "know"   con-

   jugated   (listen)

       hymn

    rap-   ture

the spear came

        shat-

tering teeth and

        brains

   folded neat-

ly   wept

    Mummy Nut

   from her star

       abode

like crystal

     falling

07-21-11

(opium)

noon
        from the Uplands seething
comes   Rumor
dressed as if and nothing more
        underscored by desire
even Legend by her wellspring
thirsts for more   white
ivy climbing   mind
        still for a while
enters the labyrinth
        of language   to kill
come down from Invention
to shadows mingling with hearsay
        chattering chittering small
bats flung against walls
    the   invisible
aorist tense   (I am aghast
        a "king" for a day)

rills of night

               and water

in all its vagaries   to drown

      style   fission

ennui in wine despond

                   seas

of magnificent distance

                    without memory

like the time of the asbestos

        angels whose wings

     enormous with pride removed

the Hour from its day

               near the shore

listing in her small bark   Isis

 a statuary

             snub-nosed

broken at the pedestal

     where grass used to grow

going in circles the mariners

     who have lost their minds

pitiful handful

                      whom Zeus smote

windowless the country church

  once a fane

                    worshippers of Red

it is heat now the

                   d r o w z y

splendor   prepare to

         sleep one inside

the other   not remembering

+++++++++++++++++++++++++++++++++++++

the notion that we are "living"

   three trillion galaxies!

out of dust generated

                 returned

like the many dead

        who outnumber us

do not recall the fine morning

   set sail with Ulysses

         or drunk by mid-day

lamenting to have ever

        touched Her

the adoration in Light of Light!

  now like rutting pigs

       tiny gods of the lintel or

bower jealous sick

          Envy

as if tossed into Vulcan's furnace

  mingled with music of all manner

 a disharmony an unsettled

     with ticket in hand

but blind as to destination

"we" are revolved and

   turned inside out

       Oblivion

must no more imagine

   to continue

++++++++++++++++++++++++++++++

an other life

      grass and spittle

wind   cliff
        between her teeth
           the Poppy

08-05-11

(the mystery)

what is love in the first degree?
is it in the bathysphere descending?
is it condemned to three life sentences?
is it in the witness box of doubt and amnesia?
is it the winter of relentless aphasia?
is it the twelve forms of planetary madness?
is it the moon with its hallucinating backside?
whiter than ever bruised and buried
beneath a weight of glosses and lies
dust storms from the beginning of time
was ever?
cupid cherubic and nonchalant
indicted for manslaughter
arcadia become a wasteland
threnodies and ululation
testifying to nothing a watery section
cut off from the whole the heart
divided into hostile afterglows

can it be summed up?

green succumbs to red

rooms come and go in a vacuum

leaving in their wake a thin

undeciphered hendecasyllable

                           burning

doors through which souls are flung

ash   cinders   accumulation

is it a residency in purgatory?

love's toss of the dice

a phone call late at night

from the Beyond

                           whose ghost

wants retribution thin throated

bleeding ichor in a dusky cancer ward

how far does it go   echoing

in the tundra of dead stars

+++++++++++++++++++++++++++++++++++

it was always "that"   an assumption

to heaven   heart pierced

"manslaughter"   in the first degree
from the first step
                    to 7th heaven

or it is distance itself
the gathered darknesses
which are beyond
or it is a symphony in red
something bursting outside
the definition of beauty
where the amalgam of celestial
or the pursuit of unwavering
blank into its window of despair
or it is the function of space
where the Lock of Bernice
just hangs isolated and frozen
as in the song   a   shaking
in the body an ague a pitch
or it is simply what you cannot
                    "know"
as ancient as the sphinx

in her corollaries of enormous sand

enigmatic   on the edge

or it is the first degree   And

7th heaven   love

a question mark in reverse a

stupendous inquiry into death

a somnolence before

or afterwards on paths of Unknown

in search of the hand's shape

the imprint on the leaf

before it falls a history

of the gorgeous mirror of Narcissus

elements of oxided metal

                    morphs of rust

waking alone on the train

as it rattles to nowhere

in a dream you keep having

you keep having

you keep having   whiteness

endless   abyss

++++++++++++++++++++++++++++++++++

the eye in its solitary condition

of being and seeing alone

takes in the entire horizon

dust settles

a man

fortunate he who in this vale walks

a dark something reaches

from above wringing color

out of his shadow

exhausts

        for a love

the existence of

isn't she beautiful?

isn't she just?

isn't she true?

        what

is the search for hemlock

at the end of a day

twilit submerged beneath immense

       water

ear in its solitary
of being to hear
                    in the first degree
she just
she true
she beautiful
                a handful of
light sparse is all it takes
a moment of creation
the expansive inordinate numeral
we are
what it is like air
                a singing
from dawn   across
appears mysteriously
for a supreme second
unable to receive it
in its entirety the human entity
scrolls down
                    symbol and cipher

before miles of desert black
          cannot go back
child,

08-12-11

(air)

who has been there, when it was
somewhere   in the
                              air
a voice a fraction
                         of time
when it was gone, then
        it was gone   some
color for a moment some
        for a moment   some
then it is gone, thinking
                              that is
for a while on earth
names like Diomedes or
                         plunging
through the hole
          the hole   netherworld
who had been there, here
          really among shades

44

possessed, really

                   the mind at best

in its collective dream

               dream   sleep-

ing a poem, where it was

             asking for words

define breath or light   words

archaic sounds   pronounced

carefully into the

              air

nothing to hold   colors

nothing to hold   air or dust

             ashes

to think that it was, where it was

passing through

          air, or

earth where the dead

     where the dead far from light

pass unkempt

           or water deepest

like night boundless waves

even stars yes, stars

because eyes have to have

something   to see

to see   some one thing

high in the

air, or

darkness

, who was here

when it was

a memory

now a memory   gone

out of time   like

air

ascending is heaven

there?

(for José)

08-28-11

(Buddha)

ancient rain, do you know me?
ancient rain, what is love?
buddha's tiny brain
a nutshell called Universe
every thought lasts forever
even love
ancient rain, do you call me?
ancient rain, what is love?
buddha's small fingers
contain the vast galactic net
stars that flash at noontime
even love

it is going away
numbed one by one
the very last thought
a lover has
going away
dew drops
buddha's archaic left hand
writing writing invisibly
the ancient rain

09-25-11

(impermanence)

    i "say it right"

when even the sun is a distant memory
             were a thousand cities
sprung like hairs in the mind
of a deity
             colossal like a father
who are to say why it is not
changes in the color red
             fundamentally
and immense towering a funnel of water
that rushed in to take the land
away from the colonizers
             the execution of Troy Davis
must drill into the collective conscious
             like jesus christ
who cannot utter anything final
             guilt and concupiscence
             a photographic likeness

who is a

       but a shadow, yes

formed out of sand a small reminiscence

       cries of children banked

in a yellow refulgence flowers mums

       walking backwards into a

longing

       such is the stellar abyss seen

from the shores of avernus

       "leave your grief and pains

          there"

how will we recall

       how will we ever remember

what it was going against the stream

into a longing

       houses stacked one

upon the other white clap-board

       dust really nothing but

a cloud of it arose at once

       a thunderous outburst

rent the sky virtually in two

so that looking from one end of the universe
to the other
                        a single conflagration
between the ears
                        smoking
consciousness levied of any attributes
            empty warehouses silos depots
            smell of pitch tar sulfur
the engine idled then died
                if someone could say
it right

            ii   "rolling in the deep"

the song's unremitting intensity
            "we could have had it all"
ashes
        as dense as the wall of eternity
lifted like a mere rope
            into the fog rolling across

the remains of the nation-state

        hate and ire tossed into a brown

paper bag

is it that we are numb?

is it that displeasure?

is it that

                  from birth

moving from one museum gallery

to the next   from birth

is it that   watching

    paintings peel from age

that we are numb

               from birth

legend of echo haunting the very green

    mariposa flutters almost invisible

wings of attitude rounding

       the cape of "good hope"

under the homicide sunne

      whose unruly head

that from birth   *we are numb*

   into the deep we are plunged

names altered by the wind
from displeasure and from afar
                lead soldiers soldered
   to the pivot of gravity
and flung by some wrathful god
                 of yore hirsute and
drunk on his parades
     among the motels of earth
from birth
          if the room is empty
          is the mind full?
when and news reaches us that still
     another death is reported
does the ear listen?
         it is the rumor of glass crashing
of enormous simulacra of men
       cracked like clay shards
of the brain struggling to think
of distance and only distance
      we are forever kept apart
it is the other we are born as

       and weeping from birth
on the dotted line
                  for whom grief
the tolling bell the atavistic dirt
      that displeasure
"we could have had it all"
              mariposa

         iii "secreto de amor"

the back-up singers
              for all the world like
angels in wild
          disheveled for the part leering
in azure outfits skin-tight keeping
      to a rhythm hypnotic dazed
and I am moved to see the moon
      once again in its orbit
though only half as much but shining
yellow   crazy

imagery of water reflecting water
on stilts as if gliding

                                        a surface of ice

compact ribbons of asphalt

                 moving from one gallery
to the next in a honeycomb maze

                   city of man

  thou dwellest in my heart *infinity*
dost perish so soon?

                           troubadours

homeless beneath undying starlight

               longing and cold
to suffer and the unknown
from another land

                             from birth

love in whose fane we all

                          do witless

go and as if in a dream

                      what is

can no more be

                  but and always

wracked and mad the heart's sailor

    shifting towards and through glass

to what outermost horizon

               longing and cold

and if I lift my gaze higher

       what celestial mansion do I espy?

avenues that go nowhere

            parallel universes

from what swart pitch do we descend?

      is it that love which

moves the farthest planet from its axis

is it that love

           longing and cold

one remove from the inch

         of passion and infirmity

is man's being

          still does another death

add to the zero

            nothing

iv "la fuerza del destino"

who then in memory moving
        as if to touch each other and recognize
but stone and depthless
sleeping
            nor do one another the self realize
but dizzy within cells of quartz
does man's soul to wake struggle
when I got the telegram
                        too late
how much weeping and on their knees
as if a different sky were watching
as if indifference   watching
streets of dust and mobs howling
        silently
    how then explain these strange lights
these night objects whirring like insects
that no mind can absorb

     in a hundred years

none of us will be here

                    but grass and

the rapt unwinding of time

through corridors the color of honey

   try to recall what we were dreaming

          in spanish

 la fuerza del destino

              one body being

exchanged for another

        one life being mistaken

for the other   berlitz lessons

the room slowly empties of all *objects*

a buddha in his ancient automobile

      goes riding through maps

of the sierra nevada looking for what is

lost looking for

        how is it that

in the end we cannot tell what

was

                la fuerza del destino

impermanence

the sudden nothingness

impermanence

suddenly light of nothingness

I hold a lamp up

                        fireflies

for a fleeting minute what lasts

        d i s s o l v e s

of impermanence

                        a light

a lume spento

                la fuerza del destino

10-03-11

(red shift)

as distance increases and
space separates from space
black backs into black
unholy and furious novae
erupt just outside mind's skin
light reddens its thin shift
until perception halves its
dimension and love recovers
nothing of its lost entelechy
tangential columns of air rise
to support heaven's blank
and throughout the body
a seismic orgasm raptures
it is nothing conscious now
too late the threadbare words
bleak mud intense darkest
woof labyrinthine discharge

buddha pastes a small lamp
in far off sri lanka where
cave people summon a deity
who will manifest as azure
and nothing that happened
before will ever happen again
but enormous thunderclaps
buried deep within sleeping
roll massive purplehead clouds
creating a summer of endless fire
who will go swimming in the magma
who will chant from peaks of sulfur
who will recite from the depths
the ineffable vedic discourse
if gods come to be chattering
in rooms that can only be empty
if gods come to be as parrots
with brilliant plumage imitating
the sounds of the echoing Nymph
whose raiment is a red shift

that threatens to vanish

no sooner is it dreamt

+++++++++++++++++++++++++

vanish no sooner do we dream

never to wake

again

10-05-11

fog over berkeley hills
fog over berkeley hills
thick and morning
not half begun before
pearly sun breaks
softly moaning
behind clouds
day light
where
it is
sea
beyond
somewhere
else

10-11-11

(the poem)

is at last not what you expected
mysteriously but inserted in air
a sequence or oblivion beauty-
fully haze and red embroidered
much before dying a breath a
recording in image of summer
's futile passage way a fiction
alive wasn't water going other
directed by a small deity fused
to sleep's unseen baggage read
for this a scansion of virgil or
his double singing latin birds
what is writing that upstairs
isn't that furious "they" ask
ignorant of memory's little
notched in the bark of an idyll
love in several books unpaginated

paragraphs of great white cloud
rain a moon dropping from
sky the indistinct smoke of
a perilous kiss somewhere near
the exit from hell gasoline
has a rhyme scheme blurred
by the nubile thing who imagines
she is the poet's romance because
in a doublet of lace and daggers
dredged the lake that is for
a shadow of her trace angry
really "they" do not recognize
it is tuesday ready for gold-leaf
life is so disappointing to die
for rounding a corner shaking
with an intuition I am not sure
what is meant by "that" hiatus
in middle old english veering
dangerously off galactic course
sun's antiquity worn like a hat

burning nevertheless burning
as are emotions that cannot
express lies down darkly a
passion fixed in liquid hate
followed by one by one a
concrete does not rupture
ars poetica properties ice
steam foliage oceanic surge
in bed with a phantom all
this time her once exquisite
now a skeleton a box of bones
smiling nether wards into dusk
a prophylactic a worm meant
meal assuaged nothing brim
to the lip can't you see it?
step around the corpse
in their stiletto heels all
perfumed the muses so-called
for their mountain trips
a vast beyond named void

expressions of do you want me
despite the divorce in late
october the rain again the
fog and the rain again forget
to turn off the stove the house
will burn anyway from afar
ulysses tied to the mast
shrill the sirens in their
see through skin lovelier
than usual at noon studying
the passage about nuclear
destruction in hexameter no
less the poem is about this
a furious misgiving with
light at odd angles a shift
red at first flirting with the
who? system collapse in delta
bifurcation which is sexual
in advance of the lyric
the song supposed to go

into ethereal how you get
high stoned on the watch
"they" go by an imaginary
street the rain again nervous
a smaller deity yet absconds
with some shadowy presence
to die like that on a tuesday
just past noon near the bush
where the aborigines count
to three before disappearing

10-18-11

(the other poem)

high-tension wires
       or in greek
  ἡ μυρι' Αχαιοις αλγε' εθεκεν
occasionally the uses of void
instead of words anger mount-
ing the perfect participle
an instance of a goddess high
on marble flashing like ingots
of pure gold between the massing
purple thunder clouds
of wretched the condition of
man groveling in his ant-heap
rain in its manifestation of
so many the summers come and gone
grammar book in hand the
flush of incognito beneath
the car chassis a calligraphy

of love the of wretched man
his state brought low by
concupiscence and adultery
sing muse Oh! delphic utterance
barely conscious the commerce
of flesh paid for by myriad
the pains inflicted on the *Αχαιοι*
sleepless on lawns of heat
do we hear the grass murmur?
moons stridently red overhead
and an invisible car roaring
through the firmament
brings to bear on the dialogue
a messenger headless with anarchy
tumbles forth like an angel
drunk and iridescent with rage
into the metal just east of
the gravel where hell's exit
was meant to be there where
pointing with his gnarled index

the resemblance to Dante
a cloth cast over the face
for yellow read perplexity
for azure divine the origins
for I have ever been heedless
falling into the raiment of Beatrice
caustic riddles of a thirteen
year old stepping out of church
how Sunday the morning!
bright and tuscan ochre
archaic burnish on the Bell
enigmatic rush between the ears
for whom stunned in bliss
I wait watching for a star
what happened to that girl?
for green scan the divinities
here among us wretched
the mortals among whom walk
spell bound with myriad the
afflicted the Argives peal

brief they lay the corpse
down on the beach as foaming
the turbulent water picks
up high its devastating wave
wine-dark and ancient
as the poem itself

10-19-11

(corydon, my heart)

the entire summer was a meadow
the bosky bower the green glens
the darkening dales & silvery rills
all echo and echoed and echoing
still your shadow that once walked
as if the whole summer a meadow were
beside what founts and gurgling springs
to betide what deity's soft hearkening
lispy whispering of nymphs unclad
intent on corydon's fluted song
he was my corydon too he was shadowing
me my echo too his rills my silvery
his bowers my bosky his glens my green
his dales my darkening especially
my darkening his footsteps in soft
underfoot persephone's secret cove
weaving image after image of ancient

his was my heart too his heart was
Mine! behind what willows beside what
streamlet led his flock to drink while
slumber the god in his raiment cool
lay grasses down for him to bed
his chilled brow his fevered lip
what mystery did my corydon cup?
what enigma dire his soul inspire?
through what leafy labyrinth did
through what aching did through
what amaze did indeed his eye alight?
in broad noon's brightest hour
espied my corydon his star blazing
in sky's farthest and aeriest mansion
of carved crystal the rooms laid bare
hush no voice dared incur a syllable
to sound though his ear all took in
and as one who has seen Beyond
as one who has seen far Beyond
how did then the Planet veer off course

taking in its troubled wake his shadow
my corydon's shadow my shadow?
how shall I another summer bear?
is there a circle that will return
my corydon to me with all his music
with all the lush variation of his music?
is there a glass into which I may peer
and see not me but him at last?
it is fate for me to walk alone now
by the fount made dry the rills parched
the glen turned to seer autumn eternal
the bower uprooted of its bosky
the dales blackened by envy's pitch
like a death living I am day after day
his death I am living day after day
would that summer a lifetime were
corydon my corydon's death I am
a myth an echo a distance a longing
a remembrance that cannot to me
him return

I am my corydon inside out
my corydon's shadow outside in
is in me the round of dreams
by turns green and fade and window
snow and timbrel and cloud
by turns all the me I can never be
in some memory's forever wanting
to be again forever wanting
to repeat being again in a shadow
cast long over the meadow guarded
by dragon flies and haunted by cicadas
the round of dreams
the drum in the heart quiet
once and for all
the drum in the heart
the drum

11-20-11

(end)

what is percent?

what is moon?

what is not?

who are the people who are here?

poets?

what is spark plug?

what is end?

what happened to the girl?

what is matter?

why?

is it snowing?

mountains followed by

mountains a way

through a way

out a way

what is distinction?

star bright on a platform

unqualified night

the Beyond

after it ends

dust whorls

burning

burning

burning

what is function?

what is middle?

what is longing?

being alone

not knowing the "other"

enigma

variations or

versions

white on

white

blank on

black

suddenly enormous

figure of a buddha

shadowless & upended

conversing with

multiplying void

standing shock still

being empty

wordlessly immense

a whole without a half

picture perfect

assumption and

what happed to the girl?

topless in a bar

one-sided

like a mirror

a vision

reading poetry

to a statue

to many statues

many many

arma virumque cano

a god at the door

wants his effigy back

listen?

a leaf falling

a single leaf

in an unlit zone

goes nowhere

sound of many

nameless shifting

through corridors

for centuries

silence

lips swollen

regret and nostalgia

too late

what is error?

blind chance

ovaries

passion

the color red

another color red

the past

unconscious presence

what is future?

what is planet?

auto-destruct

around the corner

another space

takes shape

+++++++++

zero

what is zero?

love

what is love?

(memory)

at breakneck speed

universe

green involves

distance

yellow envelopes

distance

music

(memory)

entropy

collapses

(memory)

mmm

(you)

,

10-23-11

(two poems)

i (the life)

in this monastery there are only dragonflies
from here to the mountain
the distance is measured in reflections
water shimmers somewhere below
sky sleeps as always beneath the eye
where dreaming is a fraction of all color
and the sliver of light hovers like
thought in its glass caravanserai
is it a wonder you woke up
and revealed yourself an adept
in motion and speech a being?
among all others you walked
enumerating the principle of red
undergoing and achieving sunset
in high school you were awarded
for the poem about the gilded tomb

but later in a reversal of fortune
wandering truly among the asphodel
murmuring in the language of reeds
asunder from most spatial realms
drunk in the tavern of the lovelorn
spent in the chasuble spurned &
what was the thought you were having?
labyrinthine and lunar weft a discharge
in the nocturne between keys
slowly slowly up the path worn
to the junction of sight and sound
peeling ice from the core to reveal
a soul shopping for its other
magnetize me! the statue seemed
to shout into the marble quarry
mesmerize me! as shot after shot
sent into the stellar roof amazed
missed the mark and fallen
as one already dead hit the floor
near the echo of times lost

how did it arrive then to this
monastery inhabited by dragonflies
to this rumor of living things
captured in a god's small fist
to this rut in the earth at the foot
of the mountain all dewy mist crested
landscapes of impossible distances
were you still walking?
ancient and enigmatic the quarry
out of which carved insignia
the heavens obtain their value
but you ever outside listening
unresolved a misnomer
a breathing deep within the flesh
counting down each last thought
one is ever having like you
cloud-like stunned in love with
but never consummated
inch of reason blinking
in the air which is the fiction

of a solid
of a dense
alphabet
cast to the outer ramparts
swirling   giddy
with diaphanous wings
like those of a dragonfly
you hover above a pool
reflecting
unseen

ii (the love)

cadaver thief
vagabond illusionist
what tarry here and for ever!
thrust outside the "thought"
immersed in an illegal scent
and listening for the key to click

for the door to open
for the shadow to cross
archaic and aching flowers
dispersed over the rocking floor
did you have to argue and shout?
what is so metaphysical about that?
what is the varnish for?
it's always about absolutely nothing
dalliance and opium
long drawn out afternoons in red wine
or the thick smoke of a dream
inside the dream when words
carry no weight and off course
you careen into gravity
a wreck for broken promises
coming home beyond hours
to the thing you left behind
"I promise to never again"
and always do again tongue-tied
stomach in a knot inevitably

going back to the scene of the crime
hiding in the bushes waiting
                    for love
waiting for love's lipstick
to write some bright words in the air
and you hunkering down with socrates
to discover the just and the good
dancing in an empty apartment
in the year 1959 or for that matter
the year you rediscovered fog
and the bay it assumes
with its mournful horn sounding
the just and the good
making love on a bed with three legs
writing something inscrutable
in an airplane "bodas de sangre"
about the time they turn off
the hotel lights and the garbage men
return to pick up the shadows
it is already late in the sierras

or up the coast the unnamed
a siren as much as she can sing
doubled over before traffic
unable to do it again
the just and the good
the dialogue with the "other"
creating an orient of despond
a scenery of fantastic mountains
waterfalls suspended in cloud banks
each of us is a buddha
a naked and starved remnant
obliged to compassion
hovering like dragonflies
over the pond of illusion
you for me
me for you

10-28-11

(día de los muertos)

wasn't supposed to be like this, Joe
bright autumn spectral with wind
taking the tree tops right off
a heaven is a distance too many
Joe, listening carefully to a music
cartwheels of melancholy melody
leaves as are the generations of men
beneath our feet shuffling rustling
dry voices in a dry month belonging
to void and null, Joe, not the birthday
party with the multiple-lost in their
minifold cloth of childhood's ago
not today any more not yesterday
a radio, Joe, all alone singing out
into the otherwise air beyond what
can not be grasped nor understood
why write this at all in the face
of such invisible catastrophes

just like in the photograph, Joe
when you and I on the lakeshore
what was the intention depicted?
we were already dead rehearsing
the mask of eternity with laughter
captured by a lens colored life
for just a brief second, Joe, for
an instant looking into the sun
as if futures had all been cancelled
that long day ago lost a fiction
ruminating in a philosophy book
when the already manifests
as the immutability nothing
like dancers like musicians
who have arrived too late
to play

11-2-11

(otro día de los muertos)

una muñeca libre
sin ventana ni paraguas
en el fregadero el silencio
acostumbrado de los toltecas
sin lavar sus manos dirigiendo
sus flechas hacia el ruido
de las nubes este día
sin hora ni aviso
sin zócalo sin nada sino
la masa harina de las estrellas

11-2-11

(real)

world is multiple and delusional
variable to recognize what ever
the dozen or so universes that ended
just before this one a handicap
running counterclockwise a thrill
grassy loam slope shapes darkening
before the light the one and single
penetrating to the bone the hispid
nightmare aren't you worried?
about tomorrow what is there
to say about the bride gift the
run of the mill variable and as
to recognize what is the form
in the closet the growling outside
the window the footsteps faintly
perceived before dawn an edge
at times crimson delusional a
fresh pattern to the dew this morning

world shivering in the traffic a
drizzle on the windowpane a
choking trying to suppress an emotion
crying finally but alone surrounded
by variable to understand this is
a moment like no other you reply
to the questionnaire a woman a hood
over her otherwise hair undulating
and soft reading epic fragments
before homer a theban column
in flames the text over and over again
situation and smoke alphabets
high in the air mercurial moment
when dazzled you speak to the other
who is at last the intention to vanish
etches of dun colored hills just
over the horizon a bridge to nowhere
isolated variable a world second
to the hour you are developing
to frame this color using only

opaque glass a rim of sentiment
at times spanish as the sunset of
memory searching for it that is
in the weeds behind the deserted
garage a replica of a ship in the wind
honestly you think multiple as
universes imploding in the small water
by the bedside where a hand you
are reaching for something else
if it could be a language or a tight
rope walking scared to look down
so much noise and recollection
gathered like a knot of cloth
to define it as a world delusional
staring at the wall being erected
for the purpose of dying as we all
are dying so many years ago
not for the first time either
but always trying to think through
that death in the riddle of the photo

who are laughing and the sunshine
caught in the reflection of sleep
something under the skin is
it real this world so delusional
a music box wound up and
yes the song is how many times
have you heard it beyond
an inch at a time brief measures
the notes rise high and disappear
into the ethereal the multiple &
delusional unable to apprehend
that under your feet there is nothing

11-07-11

(the body)

am I aching to die?
sky air perfect blue
am I aching to die?
home shadow long dark
was I aching to die?
sweet grass afternoon
brother beside the body
in a swoon sunspots
magnificent wind creating
gods out of sand eddies
idling rivulet's small
water like a chinese
dream a box within a
will I be aching to die?
box neatly folded within
its self a mirror without
its image reflecting back
nothing if I am not there

aching to die (acheron)
circular memory of languages
red tributaries of sound
ellipses of a past somewhere
else in time aching to die
fornicating with an olympian
just past noon in white wine
dossiers of dolorous smoke
shafts of music aimed
at the corpse's shadow
to revive nothing a souvenir
of dust and mercury
++++++++++++++++++++
is air less bitter?
is the day without its sun?
what hour can be so long?
am I aching to die?
sleeping the width of grass
beneath the drowsy specter
of the archaic Ruin

can this be the same body?

when I was without memory

when the mother in me

was without recollection

when the years revolved

outside the routine &

the host of sentences

could not create the Poem

who then was I

if not aching to die?

place this small green

under the eyelid

spin spin spin the Eye

what it sees is Beyond

what can be seen

insert this grain

inside the Ear

what it hears is Beyond

what can be heard

can this be the other body?

the nerve of history
the seedbed of words
the logos itself
these are dumb things
animals circling the shape
of the dream they are having
being beyond the Self

am I aching to die?

11-09-11

(rain)

comes a little sleeping darker
the sense of distance a fragrance
distilled from the ancient epic
when the masks of heroes opposed
the light, green verging on black
the soul absorbed in itself depths
crumbling lengths of time wet
forever down sliding sky tossed
into its inner realms a breadth
of grass weighted by supernal
dew, weren't you supposed to call?
afternoons in the nadir wilted
floral display of a face of a realm
without boundaries a limit to
language what it can and cannot
do the recognitions of space
the archaic dust still swirling
invading mind's troubled dream

about the day you disappeared
behind the mirror outside the case
glass instead of water through which
walking shadows disperse thoughts
angles made obsolete, the number
written on the wall was simply zero
a circumference around a missing
body and still the rain falling
endlessly falling over the field
falling over the lack of color sleep
indivisible sand eddying around
a deity suddenly appeared at the top
of the stairwell haunting remote a
voice like an arrow of mercury
shot through the miasma, weary
aren't you waiting for the call
to come through the old trunk line
a messenger in dun colored skin
approaching for all the world
to end his fingers articulating

the rain's nostalgic echo a small
darkening in the corner which is
the animal of consciousness
also waiting, falling endlessly
falling into another land another
history the rain ennui of patterns
embroidery of wasted emotions
semblance of fading relations
nothing certain nothing but a
mist of words incorrectly heard
a misapprehension a shivering
cartouches of fear like rain the
falling endlessly because you were
not there you were the absent one
falling endlessly out of the sky
which is not heaven nor the abode
of the olympians, if it were so easy
to describe this rain if it were
at your fingertips to spell out
disaster for the inhabitants

of planet earth the seven billion
now connected and disconnected
by illusions by mirages by enigmas
falling coming to die in the rain
speaking to phantoms of china and
india falling out of history
into a silent chronology of water
and time falling out of
why didn't you call?

11-11-11

(nibbana)

by me heard the Blessed One
in the deer park reclining him
the other and still more other
than us mendicants in repose
cessation of all sensation
as light to the eye or sound
to the ear the day was born
still as distance by me heard
informed the Blessed One
walking with calm in outside
the deer park what a day
sun on the face still alive
feeling but not feeling alone
and not alone being there
a one of us turning to stop
the wheel from turning or
into the dry river bed stepping
such is cessation of pain by

me also heard and because
an ending to every thing
whether the grass or the color
of grass or the shape of light
entering once and for all
to wake only this once and
fall by me heard never more
to arise substantive recurring
the Blessed One like a statue
in repose come no more to talk
us mendicants alone as bodies
fall away and altered states of
light moon sun and stars we
all become ash and dust outside
what is remembered no more
is recalled by me heard no more
in the deer park circling but
without the wheel outside
the law sounds an echo bright
once cessation don't wake

no more stopping all is
what wordlessly undone
no more in Indra's net
snared not this day not ever
by me heard just one day was
ago so long in Benaras as I
wandered after the steps
of the Blessed One become a
blur a stream of images
then a Bell one clear Note

11-13-11

(the dark)

lingering, who of us can escape?
lingering, who of us can desire?
escape from desire who of us can?
inside the word is the other dark
not meaning and meaning both
who can of us escape from what
time defined is time ended
world is illusion meat-house
loosened from the whole mind
evacuates its essence, lingering
pink floral displays behind glass
memory, who of us can escape?
like the time angel came hurtling
out of heaven and hit the metal
of our oncoming car, lingering
how we defined for an instant "light"
before it went away permanently
they kept appearing & reappearing

in a dream they kept beckoning
as if to linger, who of us can?
naming the "other" in the dark
suggesting that even in the grass
the dark, a second thought to
arrange the flowers in a circle
to re name the "other", lingering
who among us? darkening of
what is beyond what is not
can no more be, ascension
the translation to heaven if
world is no more, lingering
to remember if one could who
among us will? on the dotted
line a negation of history of
what has been canceled at the
door at the window pane at
whatever, who among us can?
escape from the unwritten
from the indescribable water

dormant beside the endless
sleep, there on the floor like
a dead snake like some omen
we cannot desire, and who come
rushing out of the invisible
to announce with a fragrance
in the air the very end of time
lingering, afterwards among us
who will consider the escape
from desire, who among us?
from behind where the shadow
waits to speak to become a devil
to shake with inconsolable ague
but, who come rushing out of
some inevitable debt clause
to deny the word inside which
the other word poised in dark
waits to be pronounced, a single
vowel, lingering in midair some
where indefinable but yet close
to you and me, darkening

+++++++++++++++++++++++

don't understand the anatomy,
shivering, civil disobedience
in the face of annihilation what
amounts to, lingering who of
us can escape? meaning and
not meaning, the chasm of words
the indefinable presence and
absence of, darkening, words
& outside there is only space,
evening's irreversible loss of color
the immense, darkening, twitter
of stars of animals without shape
lingering, dream, sand, black

11-19-11

("light")

ingots

       spiral-

     ling

 through

        vast

empy-

     rean

  of

       beyond

what

     gathering

  nodes

      of

sheaves

      of

   "light"

come among us

who in

      space

                walking
          dreams
                                grassy
come among us those
who have spoken
            however few
to the gods
                    one
                            each
for every
                        function
needed
            more dark
etruscan in
                        shape
        in door-
                        ways
huddling
            prayer
                        wheels

like eye-

       s

in summer

           nights

  looking

who have come

             among

        us

stars

     the   name-

less   before

    why?

          ancient

grass bound

       I am having

  techni-

        color

vast

     fabric

of   space

     interior

design

names

a   cipher

spir

a

lin

g

this is

a   -orama

of you

isn't

it?

size of

who come among

to live

us

for   brief

life

a

is

the

        "light"

stone

      breath

          hurtling

for year

      s   until

the next time

        among us

who

    have

       "seen"

+++++++++++++++++++++

memory

memory

memory

      in transit

(oblivion)

    re-

fraction   s

    leeping

having

to go

in dark

ness

for the

lamp

is

not

there

only

of

"light"

its

echo

echo

echo

11-20-11

(&space)

situations, hours of time gone
in a summer's inch of green
folded over into velvet response
cannot hear anymore what motet
in reverse, lauds, singing over
the air waves a, immense, reverie
momentum then begins to sleep
underside water words darkened
shifts red invoking the small god
of the windowsill, fornicating, a
when over and over, her hair
at first auburn then russet then
absolutely carmine, like the island
of sicily, shimmering disappearing
into the vast and outermost reaches
of space, ants, the double and his
other exchanging mirrors because
the invisible, perplexity, each after

the same girl, the one in juxta-
position the one in cadaverous
see through, if one is dead, if
the double, not understanding
air nor the quality of light and gas
emanating from the moon tonight
nor why so many have gathered
to watch, space, the empty, mind,
reflux, totem, agitating superficially
hand in hand, comb, glass persons
somewhere on the other side of time,
natalie wood, how many years,
a mystery, hair-do beehive style,
gypsy dancing, into whose eyes
what face remains, gearing up for
a launch to orbit, planetary con-
sumption, the end in bright filigree
and denim, her, wanting, wanting
even more, to expound on theory
of the universe in quetzal or sumerian

without the anatomy to understand,
it, her drowned, a mistake near
the banks of the Lethe, where grassy
knolls invite the shepherd paris
to fuck helen, and upstairs where
most of the stars keep their ornaments
from rusting, where the black hole,
where eventually everything goes
rushing through itself, to get outside
the self to explore with the eye all
that is left of space, all that remains
of the enormous nothing, not begin
not end, ear takes in what it can
of that vague incessant roaring
in the evening grass, then body
goes down, sleeps, a small motor
+++++++++++++++++++++++++++++
not waking, not even later when
getting up to consult the map and
with no memory of what went before,

just a few stains, sex, infinite color
going out like dust, absorbed by
an exorbitant pointillism on the verge
of, dizzy, her, a mouth opens for
the intense jet of water, somewhere
else, it is no time at all

11-21-11

(longing)

the dark opposition, mountain,
that is sleeping forever now a
silence just as dark the intense
just past the thin white border,
we regard, infinite horizons or
a water that cannot subside at
the origin of things, being in
dialect a summation but dreaming
only, absence, not plenitude that
fills the opaque pronoun, who
that can be rounding the corner,
invisible, a deity poised to select
the next death among us, at odds
with the color that defines "beyond"
with the shape in the pool of night,
we are, drowning, losing breath,
groping for light, night, unawares
followed by a suite of musick
ancient and ineffable, shepherds

and rocks, distances, flutes
played in the phrygian mode,
vanishing, as we are, neither form
nor substance, a language tenuous
as the very air, unintelligible
the perhaps, and in great schemes
of meter and height a poetry
resonating, by turns echo and
memory, or its lack, pale shadows
paler still, to search for a hand
for something, anything at all
that still has touch, surfaces fade
into the mirror's nothingness
just as names disappear from
+++++++++++++++++++++++++
mind, tense, sight, depth, or
in gyres of dust circling the ever,
those who once peopled our city,
the noetic one, now themselves
returned to the sublime ache,

longing, enigmatic and undefined
like the stone that whitening
appears so abruptly on the road
we traverse dumbfounded during
the Hour, to imagine it has meaning
erect and uncreated, stone, sense
of loss, regret, endlessly rocking
in the ear's attic, dense and blank
if we could only, given a text to read
but cannot, glyphs wavering
on the distant page, logos,
a tale about thought, slender
and sleight. but cannot, no,
just the stone, within, symbols
that demand light that remain
as always meaningless, sand
and remnants of space,
longing

11-23-11

(enigma)

at the door a goddess, nose-bleed,
vomiting, memory loss, a goddess
shedding white light and wet tresses
descriptor and deictic particles,
bodily functions gone awry, middle
language phenomena especially
phonetic decay, a goddess at the
door, empty shopping bags, hectic
the look in her eye, a door, a window
where discomfited a distant land
becomes even more so, forgetting
to use honorific pronoun, forgoing
use of tongue, dazed, a door, a shade
fixed crooked over an eye, her eye,
in what year did we lose mother?
what was the event that led to
father's death? drinking heavily
invoking shiva, thinking about

the mountain and how to get there,
in her absence a door opens by itself
and the floor gives way, gnomes and
small black demons, some shouting
in the background, tinsel, flecks of
white stuff drifting, a goddess her
nakedness less apparent, like rain
her aura, did we know how to work
the motor by the bed? how to get
there in the dark, the destroyed park
trees mown down by an invisible,
it's the fear, deity, about the mountain,
invoking shiva, his consort, their
children if any, drinking heavily
before the loss of mother, foliage
draped in ceremony by the window,
at the door a goddess, again, who
can imagine a better way, who are
by now consumptive or dead, who
can understand distance, at last,

the fierce longing before sleep,
as ever, ending a day in a fit, to
have appeased the goddess, her
doorway, the great sacral element
known as sky, is it diminished?
nose-bleed, oblivion, bedside trust
broken by red shift, words in chinese
for the simplest numbers, memorizing
the words of the buddha, vomiting,
over and over, decay of final consonants,
when did we lose brother? on what
byway in what dusty province?
words of the buddha, repetition &
formula, how the colors get mixed
and start to go away in a storm, at
the door or beside it a goddess, shadows
which are a measure of time, other
people in other rooms somehow talking,
a bowl passed around, vomit and sputum,
understand nothing of evolution,

of concupiscence, of the first writings,
outside a red wind gathers all its strength
battering the tiny cities by the lake,
becoming dead, yellow, ochre, beige,
a goddess, concupiscent, at the door,
not knowing where to turn, what light,
strangers each of us, hampered by shame
forgetting the honorific pronoun,
drinking heavily, becoming dead again,
sky, small distantly bright celestial
phenomena japanese in origin, love,
a broken bridge, unfinished stairs
when did we lose brother?

11-24-11

(tree)

look at that beautiful tree
how can anyone not look at
that beautiful tree how can
it's all around us life it's all
around the beautiful tree how
can anyone not look at it
red russet ochre orange
its leaves iridescent in autumn
light in autumn light so how
can anyone not notice and
sense it life is all around
the air is fragrant despite
carbon emissions and un-
sanitary things here and
there so beautiful the tree
alone to itself a thing a
perhaps a soul anyone yes
cannot but know it is a soul

this autumn afternoon all
around us life iridescent
everything somehow lifting
above into air autumnal
light between us only space
between us images that waver
disappear are really nothing
a slant of light a perception
you were alive a year ago
once and talking walking
past this beautiful tree
across the street is the restaurant
where we last ate together
you of course remember
ten years ago it was then
on shattuck avenue near
cedar street and the green
that divides shattuck is where
the beautiful tree its leaves
red russet ochre orange

is almost scintillating can't
you see it how it is all around
life a soul is nearby you can
feel it a soul it is in the black
man playing the flute nearby
first it was "tico tico" then
a piece by bach in the light
where you were walking with
me ten years ago on shattuck
but are sleeping now aren't you
sleeping as only ash can sleep
in the deep beyond where
things begin or even have
a notion of becoming
of becoming light all around
the beautiful tree all around
the riddle of light of life
a memory all around is
how can one not notice
it the beautiful tree offering

itself to the air to the light

all around us is

is

11-27-11

(dense)

this intense, what gathers folding
in mid-air just as the light, precious
more than substance, that dissipates
in the cloud-sequence, distance
beyond sleep, beyond the seven
seas, beyond childhood's library,
intense this, dense woof of light
and distance, falling ever falling
from one body to the next, cloud-
sequence nirvana, this intense,
what unfolds gracefully in sky
unseen, the other side of the skin,
this intense unwinding, felt how
many times before, not now, unsaid
undone, falling unconsciously from
the one body, who will say which
is the next body, who will say what
memory goes with it, falls with it,

to where in the frail somewhere,
the antipodes, where angels gather,
this intense moment, looking to
the undefined, distance, unwinding
through the myriad parallel selves,
red, orange, bright green like grass,
yellow, diminishing voiceless, failing
to sound at last, leaves taken in a gust
of air, the wind, which in its immensity
shapes the dark building, the dense,
where shadows interpret the other,
where footfalls echo, where nothing,
it is this intense, this dismemberment
of ash, floating, still, the dark edifice,
labyrinthine, doubling endlessly in
the soul's search, unwinding, haunted
as are men in their sleep, dreaming
it was, dreaming some dense thing,
configuration of stars, exploding
noiselessly in the ear, liquid gold
draining from the source, you and

I, coming to be on a winter afternoon,
you and I in the childhood library,
reading to each other the tale, endless
the tale, soul's fate, recognizing in this
intense, this unfolding unwinding,
spirals of light, distance, you and I,
memory, what cannot be touched,
memory, what is dense, color of
summer, secret streets unfolding
on a secret map, sands, water,
sunsets etched in ivory, continents
of silence, then cold, the intense
dense, memory, the dark building
you and I, the dark building
+++++++++++++++++++++++++++
labyrinthine, as ash is,
spirals of light,
sky, dense,
hush

12-02-11

(distance)

at the end of all things
by which we mean melancholy
is the mountain always distance
is the street unnamed going
into some dusty dream
is the music without signature
the woods and horns slowly
dying in a sleep of beyond
misty waterfalls painted
against the ancient sky
of all things at the end
inky dusk descends at last
the mountain never reached
the sea never traversed
waves of night engulf time
and time swallowed by time itself
leaves no memory no echo
in the imagined swirl of things
ending without history

so too all men have an ending
who never reached the mountain
nor crossed the stormy sea
who have dreamed of china silk
and waterfalls on painted fans
who have never left the house
but dwelled in darkness ever
thinking in the glass to see
the life of color shape & sound
life poured into the ear
life gleaming in the eye
who have never found out
how to say the thing desired
without destroying the thing desired
and in the passage of time
have longed ever to seek the light
have longed to find the source
but in the dark have ever dwelled
sleeping the sleep of reason
but not waking unless to discord
the sound of chaos and blazing

smoky inferno of the heart
then to plunge like mites
into the forever abyss
++++++++++++++++++++++++++
how is it you and I
living in the world of men
the self-same dream shared
the light and source to find
eked out this little time
at once so close in the end
so distant
as far from the mountain
as far from the painted waterfall
as light is from the unfathomed
++++++++++++++++++++++++++
loss of the thing desired
loss of the thing unfound
(were you the one on the right
or the left of distance?)

12-04-11

(penumbra)

light falling less now
patterns not as distinct
tradesmen like embryos
chatter using words
like "freedom" and "choice"
the god of small floors
arrives in his cups
blazoned with the inferno
of manifest destiny
do we too live diminished
in the area of despond
and lack? live unmitigated
the lesser of higher entities?
what dream was it by
the window we sought
to interpret using books
as if they were magi?
counting to excelsior

numbering the spaces
remaining before all
matter would vanish
pretending to love
the goddess of distance
as if she were a mere woman
did we not shame the air
whose holy redundancies
we never rightly understood?
come away from this
shibboleth of learning
from this sand castle
of idiom and dialectic
pretending to love
and love only the goddess
of mirror images
when it was entangled
darkness in the shape
of carnal knowledge
that possessed us

Brother, I address the boat
that has taken you away
but it too flees into waters
that bear no reflection
Brother, I seek in wood
the sculpted arhats
whose divinity gives
direction to thought
and hence thought to
nothingness even though
sleeping it seems bright
and with form and
meaning as if such
distinctions mattered
in the world of ash
and Brother, I let loose
each hand at last
grass stained and now
gnarled with years
knowing they can no

longer bring you back
no longer take your
shadow and place it
exactly where mine
stands slowly dissolving
in the penumbra

12-05-11

(memory)

a solitary egret standing
in a marsh of russet grass
far from the poem
a monument however blind
        to the emperor
a hole in the air
notwithstanding a fan
held by an invisible hand
rushing to announce
                what happened
years ago eons ago
or never at all but in dreams
        the imperial wall
a congestion of people and dust
green stains on glass
        whose face
in the mirror staring back
into the palindrome of history

before darkness

       descends like a curtain

over the cliff beyond

where an inscription now

effaced remains as a puzzle

for no one

           suggested

a troubadour mounted

in the first rays of the sun

sings the lark

             ancient

notes hanging in a golden

panoply of atmosphere

     to recall even

the semblance of that grammar

motley particles dissolving

        sinuously

          in faint columns

         of wind

12-11-11

(forgets)

impossibility of night
a horizon of 14 different idioms
speaking the language of pearls
in the magnificent depth
of the stellar sea
dreams awash in coral sifting
through designs of nostalgic
distances each as far from the self
as the self from its death
and to know just once
being alive between the ears
and seeing really seeing the divine
point where reflection turns outwards
beyond the skin of identity
outwards towards the ink of time
irretrievable to know just once
breath and light at the core
as if to turn again

around the little god of grasses
into a childhood absence
into   sleep as dark
as the life that went before
knowing suddenly how death
inhabits the person from the start
how divined in the photograph
the shadow already takes flight
from   eyes focused
                semblances of air
   nothingness   hole in   sky
out of   angels felled
summon   daily catastrophes
impossibility   night
horizon   desire
unfulfilled   longing
languages of   silence
does   Wheel take us
from   unmixed water
into   cloud   forgetting?

all around   hands of small beings

pray for   admission

but what is to   grasp?

          is to   hold?

does   verb employ

archaic   forms

          new   tongues

longer   deeper

          before   time

 forgets

                    oblivion's

crimson   thread

                    never

                         un-

winding

          a

            the

12-17-11

(charon)

much lights less the dwindling
winter day how
                    a fog entering
the house darkened from inside
nothing   sleeping fire
steps unheard a passage
to myth   cycles
on her head the blazing crown
              of dreams
pitched face down into
                          inferno
sage and marjoram
                        a touch
by the small beaker
meant to summon the sea from its
immense and wrathful bed
moon   drawn and haggard
snows a little hummock

tilled the hard dirt
with a nail   rust
lessened by a half   sky
who can announce the bright
standing shock still

                            the wavering
pillar of hair
                     how much did you
learn about the advent
                     you learn
siding with the revolutionary forces
frost-bitten   piece-meal con-
                     fession   sobbing
into the soiled pillow where
          sex at least 15 times
before re winding the tape
                where it says
"I have ever though never having
seen you loved   you"
abyss   to answer

to the cold to the
           inside the house
fog   "brumaire"   clouds
taking away the breath
           where the inert
a body   beneath
wrapped in yellowed sheets
porphyry and onyx
a handful of worn byzants
          to cross
to the other shore
being sure to tip the wary
         boatman

12-17-11

(historia)

piedra terciaria aullando
mas sin dios pero siempre
con agujeros celestiales
cacayamando mayaztecas
en asuntos bipolares mixta-
textatoltecastísimos o mejor
dicho merodeando bajo palabra
respiración toda al lado cristal
dos veces más furiosa que antes
en fuego circular añadido al
diente lunar del transatlántico
siguiendo su mapa de chorros
animales fluorescentes o no
sin el mínimo alrededor emperador
carlos extincto cuerno de aceituna
vertido en vasos humeantes apenas
descubiertos dentro de los sesos
más trotzkistas improbables con
el funfun ronron chichicastenango
de un domingo en la alameda de
las pulgas con miedo asustado
por el abuelo de las máscaras
ay qué porvenir sin ruedas
asfaltadas arabigofuniculares

corazón de mi pachuco
tatuado en brazos planetarios
devolviendo su tabasco
hasta el milímetro infernal
de un méxico todavia inacabado
de inventar!

12-18-11

(echo)

until you can endure no more
and when light comes full circle
and the probabilities of love
are no longer endless but finite
as the space allotted to the deity
who governs the top of the stairs
until you can bear no more
the whip-lash alphabet of fate
when the star-probe ushers in
the catastrophe of the end
and the possibilities of love
have vanished in a semaphore
of water and night when and
and only then the syllable "red"
corresponds to the fateful day
of a labyrinthine rhetoric
when brick equals marble
like the total inferno of memory

pitched on its timeless wheel

then witless with exhaustion

do the parameters of love cease

and outside the flimsy firmament

of the hundred thousand galaxies

the worm of reason goes mad

devouring and being devoured

in the incessant dream of passion

instantly reduced to a thimble

of thought convulsed and aching

because the window is not there

because the door has been removed

and the floor where the body lies

burns with a momentary idea

that heaven is a piece of torn silk

bound to the mouth of Echo

who herself mirrored in a perfume

of non-existence ceases to sound

++++++++++++++++++++++++++++

it is not being

     it is not being

it is not being

for everywhere and nowhere

love's shattered relic clings

to the artificiality of recall

that limbo of dazed yellow perfection

that nostalgia of green cataracts

pouring through the eye of the Beloved

who in coming to be surrenders

all possibility of ever loving again

is this what you mean by "death"?

is this what you mean by "immortality"?

it is a music of instant starts and

finishes by being nowhere

flush eternity of orgasm

a million cycles of light

going backwards into "red"

going backwards

like light coming full circle

in the little grass of myth

that suddenly appears

on the paper like a kiss
to be dissolved when the flame
yields to the moth
becoming ash
ascending
air

12-19-11

(world)

world? what world?
we move from the room of Beauty
to the room of the Potentially dead
on the left the etruscan graffiti
denoting either the labors of herakles
or the harrowing of hell
on the right the Ditch of shadows
where the silent struggle with the silent
for a chance of light
for a chance to move forth
out of the mausoleum
out of the museum
into the world of semblances
into the world of distance and mountain
where the sun of day with its myriad motes
sets love on its wheel for the instant
of recognition and oblivion
sets love into the air a bird aloft

out of the mausoleum
out of the museum
"eripe me domine"
on the left the etruscan graffiti
on the right the Ditch of shadows
which world? "their" world?
potentially dead moving from
the room of Beauty
into the much denser atmosphere
musk incense burning visions
of the holy river teeming with pyres
fire floating on water
air a-swarm with angels half alive
set love like a bird aloft
"their" world shifting from red
into the realm of dark matter
where atoms no longer exist
where the sleeping world goes
when it is exhausted from accidence
and the triviality of lesser deities

who have lost all governance
do we hear wailing?
world? which world?
neon incandescence of endless streets
bonzes in torn saffron robes
on their knees making their way
to the temple of Avalokishetvara
everyone else going the other way
into the perfume of purgatory
little fir branches in their fists
"eripe me domine"
+++++++++++++++++++++++++
what day is it in the world?
is it the hour of breaking bread?
is it the minute of redemption?
on the left etruscan graffiti
on the right the Ditch of shadows
where someone is buried every 10 seconds
"La Madre del Amor Hermoso"
who watches over us as we make passage

158

from this world to the next
I have the chills today
falling in and out of consciousness
in what year are we in ancient Florence
under the bridge the sluggish Arno
to meet with the goldsmith Cellini
the swallows make a great swoop
above the Duomo
there are those for whom pain is all
for whom no other thought exists
married to the rain of despair
or who suddenly encounter in the noise
a former lover who has not aged
these hundred years wearing silver foil
to hold the mass of bright red hair
do not remember how that ended
from this world to the next
which world?

+++++++++++++++++++++++++++++++

moving from the room of Beauty

to the room of the Potentially dead

which we are all waiting

for the summons

and outside aloft the bird takes flight

the love of a moment

with wings of air

singing into the dark

oncoming Cloud

singing

12-24-11

(silent)

you never know when
nor why if when crossing
the golden plain in search
of whatever dusty dream
in childhood aroused you
to make a noise and joy
to learn sanskrit at dawn
today not really matters
if the bird in the cage
what a song dispels air
catch what you can of
the intensity clearing a
bed for the body finally
clouds enter the room
what a single hour contains!
a love letter written as
if eternity were the next
hour to be followed by

red shift into blue dark
overwhelms silence a note
sifted through foliage
rising ascending reaching
for the source of light
interspersed by cities
transparent as onion skin
machines great oil slicks
marshes dumps dead lakes
eternity stretches after
into the desert of time
no one can remember
exactly what or why
it was significant event
a crowning or jewel theft
watching a human
plunge into distance of water
a sole entity in wonder
as pass sky and nebulae
through the distraught eye

how much azure cloth
patched to the hand
waking it was a few
minutes later amazed
at the size of death
like a mountain of ash
silently

12-26-11

(a day in the sun)

I promised to take Mom to Brazil
but she thought you were more spiritual
both of us at once talking at the same
time with the same voice
sitting on folding chairs
at the improvised patio table that
dad had painted orange below the
weeping willow below the immense
shadow that we ignored was there
up the street there was a map convention
laid out on a large summer lawn
most of them had purple covers
and spread out we watched dazed
as the yellow boulevards sinuously
made their way from one big city
to another pretending that somehow
we inhabited any one of them
all the time which was better than living

where we did watching carefully
how the lizard traced its course
across the gravel into how much light!
what was true was not necessarily
the right proportion of love
nor the sudden manner in which the years
took us away from each other
from that day in the sun dizzy
with the sheer instantaneity of it
all I mean all and forever
in and out of the same skin "being"
alive grass rushing to be cut
sidewalks crazy for us to step on them
school kids shouting into the evening
the early warnings about dying
the taste of bitumen at the bottom
of the swimming pool where we plunged
eager to swim into some asian apocalypse
to re-emerge wet and drunk
for a single morning waving sweetly

some imaginary record into the sun
the song which laced our ears
with the promise of pyramids
and crowded marketplaces far far away
all I mean all and forever
mexican shirts of fantasy
the two of us disappearing
into a movie theater
dark and endless

12-29-11

(songs)

joe, last night
Nat King Cole and Peggy Lee
came by
             he sang "unforgettable"
and Peggy sang "fly me to the moon"
             and "I'll be seeing you"
her voice was so ethereal and she wore
a big red dress and a silver thing
around her head, joe
and Nat was as cool as ever
       I felt your presence right
next to me, we were in the 9th grade
waiting for the dance,
                           waiting
for Jo Stafford to come by
and sing "you belong to me",
joe, that was our favorite one
       made us feel so innocent

and far away like we would never
   be again,

                never be again

02-03-12

AFTERWORD:

A Day in the Sun reads like a flowing symphony of universal resonances plucking the strings of the human heart before transporting you through the mythic realms and then into the cosmos in a timeless and haunting kaleidoscope of imagery.

In tribute to his twin who entered the Great Unknown, Ivan Argüelles masterfully weaves his words around the axis of the Great Mystery with its constant motion of existence and nonexistence, known and unknown. Many universal truths are revealed and then hidden again.

This collection explores the themes of impermanence and human paradox that at once reads as part Zen koan, part cosmic philosophy, and part beat poet with a touch of surrealism: "We were already dead rehearsing the mask of eternity with laughter." Or "if the room is empty then is the mind full?"

Like a cosmic shaman, Argüelles uses the instrument of language to transmute human emotion, creating a subliminal effect that offers new ways of linking ourselves to our existence while opening fresh horizons of perception. At some points you can almost hear the ancient flute of Kokopelli opening the secret gate into the sipapu taking you on a journey between the worlds before dropping you back to earth again.

Pure genius!!

Stephanie South, wife & biographer of José Argüelles